TRUE STORIES • HIDDEN FACTS

FAMOUS MYSTERIES

Anita Ganeri & David West

WAYLAND
www.waylandbooks.co.uk

CONTENTS

INTRODUCTION

Huge, ape-like creatures. Lost cities of gold, ghost ships and UFOs, monsters living in Loch Ness. For centuries, people have been puzzled and fascinated by famous mysteries like these. Some can be explained by science; others remain unexplained. Their stories make gripping reading as their hidden and baffling facts unfold.

LIFT THE FLAP
TO FIND OUT MORE

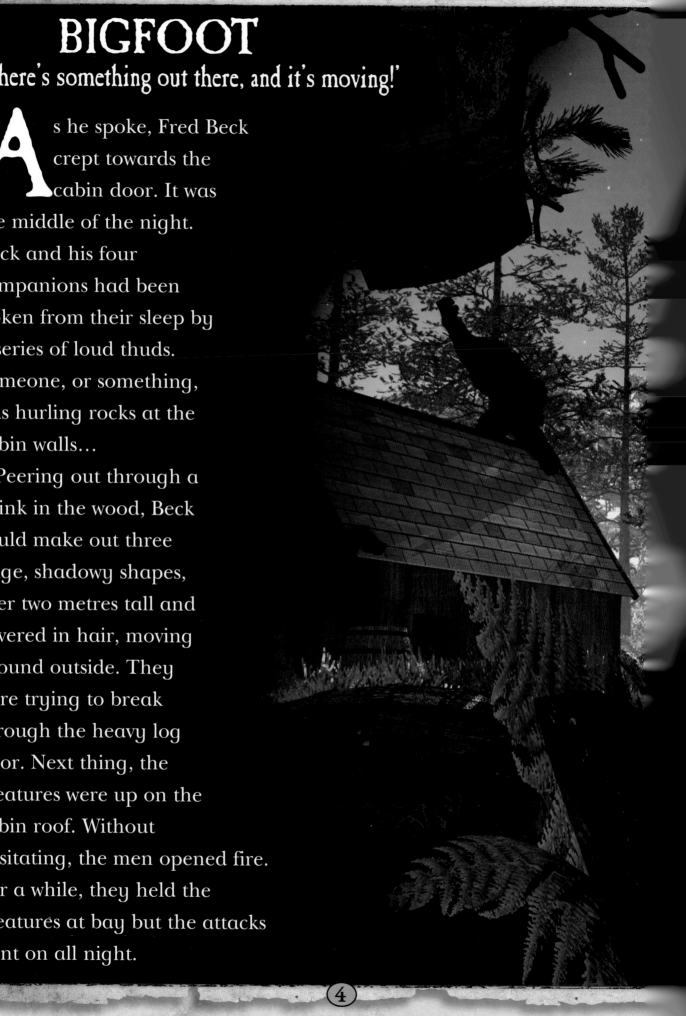

BIGFOOT

'There's something out there, and it's moving!'

As he spoke, Fred Beck crept towards the cabin door. It was the middle of the night. Beck and his four companions had been woken from their sleep by a series of loud thuds. Someone, or something, was hurling rocks at the cabin walls…

Peering out through a chink in the wood, Beck could make out three huge, shadowy shapes, over two metres tall and covered in hair, moving around outside. They were trying to break through the heavy log door. Next thing, the creatures were up on the cabin roof. Without hesitating, the men opened fire. For a while, they held the creatures at bay but the attacks went on all night.

It was July 1924. The men were miners, prospecting for gold in the Muddy River, in Washington State, USA. For days, the men had been aware that they were being watched.

One morning, as they got ready to leave, Beck suddenly turned round. Behind him stood a large, ape-like creature. Beck picked up his gun and took aim…

LIFT THE FLAP
TO FIND OUT MORE

'Gnnngh! Go, Gonzalo! We will hold them off!'

ith these words, the Spanish soldier fell forwards into the river, an Indian arrow in his back. He was one of a handful of men, led by conquistador, Gonzalo Pizarro, who had spent months fighting their way through the jungle, their dream of finding El Dorado shattered…

When he left his base in Quito, Ecuador, in February 1541, Pizarro had high hopes of finding the fabled Inca city whose walls and streets were said to be lined with gold. Its king was a great warrior, called El Dorado, the 'Golden Man'.

When he reached the valley of Zumaco, a month after setting off, Pizarro was joined by his cousin, Francisco de Orellana. The two men, together with their expedition force of more than 200 Spaniards and 4,000 natives, headed for the foothills of the Andes Mountains. At first, they made good progress but the going got steadily tougher. Worse still, when they finally reached the other side, there was nothing to see but jungle.

By now the men were exhausted and supplies of food were running low. Reluctantly, Pizarro was forced to stop and send de Orellana on ahead, with 50 of his men, to find food.

Weeks went past but de Orellana did not return, and Pizarro's men were dying. With his expedition in tatters, and no sign of El Dorado to be found, Pizarro and the remaining 80 men headed home.

The search was later taken up by the Spaniard, Don Antonio Sepulveda. In 1580, he reached Lake Guatavita where an extraordinary ceremony was said to have taken place. Each year, the local king was coated in gold dust and rowed on a raft to the centre of the lake while the crowd threw golden offerings into the water. Hoping to find the treasure, Sepulveda tried to drain the lake but the channel he dug collapsed.

Four hundred years later, a British gold mining firm decided to take up the challenge…

LIFT THE FLAP TO FIND OUT MORE

THE LOCH NESS MONSTER
'Och no, the legend is *true* – it is the monster!'

As he picked himself up off the ground, Arthur Grant could not believe his eyes. In front of him rose a huge creature with a long neck and tail. It turned its head to look at Grant, then disappeared into the dark waters of Loch Ness…

Grant, a veterinary student, was riding home early one morning in January 1934, when the massive monster slithered across the road in front of him, heading towards the Loch. Swerving to avoid it, Grant fell off his motorbike. Unhurt, Grant continued on his way home, eager to tell his story.

Grant was not the first person to see the monster. There had been many sightings reported over hundreds of years but since the lake-shore road had been built the previous year, the sightings had become more frequent. Soon, monster-hunters were arriving from all over the world to track down the creature.

In 1970 an American scientist used hydrophones to make underwater recordings of many sounds that couldn't be explained away by known aquatic creatures. Then, later in the 1970s, another team of American scientists took photographs showing what looked like a giant flipper. Was this finally proof that the Loch Ness Monster was real?

LIFT THE FLAP
TO FIND OUT MORE

THE MYSTERY OF BALL LIGHTNING

'Look out! That light, it's heading straight for you!'

As he shouted the warning, the man could see that it was already too late. The strange ball of white and blue light, which was about to knock him unconscious, had already hit his colleague on the forehead, killing him instantly.

The dead man was Professor George Richmann, a brilliant scholar and head of the physics department at the Academy of Sciences in St Petersburg, Russia, who was carrying out pioneering work in electricity. Inspired by Benjamin Franklin's recent experiments into the nature of lightning, Richmann had invented a device for attracting lightning during a storm. A wire was attached to the top of his house, leading down to an iron bar inside.

It was 6 August 1753, and the experiment was underway, when the ball of fire appeared and struck Richmann. The unfortunate professor had become the first person to be killed by a mysterious phenomenon, known as ball lightning.

But Richmann's wasn't the first close encounter. On 21 October 1638, a church in Devon was almost destroyed by a large ball of fire which smashed pews and windows during afternoon service, and filled the building with thick, dark, foul-smelling smoke. Four people died and many others were injured.

Many more accounts followed. Natural ball lightning is unpredictable and appears infrequently. It has even been seen inside submarines and on board aircraft. In 1984, the passengers and crew of a Russian aircraft had the fright of their lives while flying across the Black Sea during a thunderstorm. A glowing ball of light appeared in the cockpit, then disappeared, only to re-emerge in the cabin where it floated slowly over the heads of the stunned passengers.

The question is: what is ball lightning and how does it happen?

LIFT THE FLAP
TO FIND OUT MORE

THE ROSWELL INCIDENT
'One thing's for sure, they're not from *this* world...'

As the man stared down at the ground, shivers ran down his spine. The ghostly, wide-eyed body was like nothing he had ever seen before. With its large head and pale, hairless skin, it was definitely not human, but what else could the creature be?

All around lay hunks of twisted metal. Clearly, some sort of craft had crash landed. Quickly, Major Jesse Marcel, of the Roswell Army Air Field, ordered the site to be cleared. No one was to know about this. If any of the men were asked, they had seen nothing.

Days before, strange lights had been sighted in the skies above Roswell, New Mexico, USA. Then, eyewitnesses reported seeing one of them come crashing down. Was it an alien spacecraft? The news spread like wildfire. On 8 July 1947, anxious to keep the exact site secret, the US airforce issued a press release confirming the rumour – they had recovered a crashed 'flying disk'.

Meanwhile, the mystery of the 'alien' creature remained. In total secrecy, the body was taken to Roswell Air Base where it was kept in a hangar. Later, in the base infirmary, an autopsy was carried out…

In the following years, the Roswell Incident was declared dead. Witnesses were silenced and evidence suppressed. Would the American people ever know the truth?

LIFT THE FLAP
TO FIND OUT MORE

LOST IN THE BERMUDA TRIANGLE

'Zzzzzt...calling tower. This is an emergency. We seem to be lost.'

Flight leader, Lieutenant Charles Taylor's voice sounded strained, and the radio operator back at Fort Lauderdale had trouble making out his words. As the operator tried to find out Taylor's position, it became clear that Taylor and the rest of Flight 19 were in trouble. Seconds later, Taylor could be heard again. Then the radio went dead…

A few hours earlier, at 14.00 hours, the five US Navy torpedo bombers of Flight 19 set off from Fort Lauderdale, Florida. It was 5 December 1945. The weather was good and the routine training flight, which would take them out over the Atlantic ocean before returning to the naval base, should have lasted for around two hours.

At first, everything went as planned. The planes reached the area known as the Hens and Chickens Shoals, and started bombing practice. A short time later, they began to turn west for the second part of the test. At 15.45, the first signs of trouble appeared and problems with the planes' compasses were reported. It was hard to establish radio communications on the training frequency because of atmospheric interference. Becoming more and more disorientated, it wasn't long before the pilots were hopelessly lost.

A last radio message was heard at 19.00 hours, and two seaplanes were sent out from Fort Lauderdale to search for Flight 19. Air bases, aircraft and merchant ships were also alerted.

Meanwhile, the stricken pilots were still miles from landfall with no idea which direction they were heading in. They had no choice but to keep flying for as long as their fast-dwindling fuel supplies lasted…

LIFT THE FLAP
TO FIND OUT MORE **FATE**

MYSTERY OF THE MARY CELESTE

'Vanished – the whole crew, as if taken by the wind.'

As he spoke, Oliver Deveau shook his head in puzzlement. He had searched every inch of the ship, from stem to stern, but there wasn't a soul on board. The ship was in perfect condition but the whole crew had vanished without trace…

It was 5 December 1872. Deveau was chief mate on the Dei Gratia, a British ship sailing across the North Atlantic. When a look-out spotted a ship in trouble, heading towards the Straits of Gibraltar, Deveau and two shipmates rowed over to help.

The name of the stricken ship was the Mary Celeste. Launched in Canada in 1861, rumour had it that this 31 metre brigantine was jinxed. Tragedy struck when her first captain fell ill and died, and, from then on, disaster followed disaster. In November 1872, she was sailing from New York, bound for Genoa in Italy, when disaster struck once more.

On board, Deveau searched frantically for any sign of life. But the Mary Celeste was like a ghost ship. Strangely, in the sailors' quarters, the crew's belongings were still in place. Stranger still, the captain's table was laid with the remains of his breakfast. It was as though the whole crew had suddenly decided to abandon ship. But where had they gone?

LIFT THE FLAP
TO FIND OUT MORE

THE TUNGUSKA EVENT

'Two suns – why are there two suns?'

Shielding their eyes from the blinding light, the couple stared at the sky in disbelief. Seconds later, a massive explosion threw them to the ground. All around them, rocks and trees were falling. Was this the end of the world?

It was 30 June 1908. In the remote Tunguska region of Siberia, another hot, dry day was just beginning. Suddenly, a huge ball of bluish light flashed across the cloudless sky, leaving a trail of smoke behind it. Then the ball exploded, with a bang like gun fire.

The couple were not the only people to witness this extraordinary event. One man described seeing the sky split in two, then cover the forest in fire. By now, the heat was so ferocious, it felt like his shirt was on fire. Above, great claps of thunder rumbled and a howling, hot wind blew the man off his feet. Then, the earth itself began to move, shaking the trees and buildings…

The explosion ripped through the forest, flattening millions of trees over a huge area of land. And, for weeks afterwards, the skies above the village of Tunguska glowed with light, even at night.

But what had really happened on that fateful morning? Were local people right? Did the explosion mark the beginning of the end of the world?

LIFT THE FLAP
TO FIND OUT MORE

A GHOSTLY WARNING
'Wh-who are you? What do you want?'

Lord Dufferin's voice shook as he spoke these words. As the shadowy figure in front of him turned, Dufferin found himself recoiling in horror. The face he was looking at was so hideous, it was surely not human?

A diplomat and adventurer, Dufferin was staying at a friend's old manor house near Tullamore in Ireland. One night, he was woken up by noises in the garden outside. Looking out of the window, he saw a mysterious, hooded figure carrying a large box on his back. The figure looked up at him and stared for a moment before continuing on his way across the lawn. Thinking it must be a burglar, Dufferin went outside to investigate. As he got closer, he noticed that the box was a coffin…

Next morning, Dufferin told his friend what had happened. Both men were mystified, but decided they should put the experience down to a bad dream.

Some years later, Lord Dufferin was attending a diplomatic function at the Grand Hotel in Paris. Along with several of his companions, he crossed the lobby to the newly-installed elevator, the hotel's pride and joy.

As the elevator doors opened, Dufferin let out a loud gasp. The lift operator was the same man he had seen all those years before in Ireland! Dufferin stepped back in shock, startling his companions who had noticed nothing wrong. Then he waved the elevator to go on without them. Seconds later, the lift cables broke and the elevator plummeted to the ground, killing everyone inside…

An investigation launched into the accident revealed that the lift operator had only been hired that morning, while the regular operator was off sick. But who was the mysterious man?

LIFT THE FLAP
TO FIND OUT MORE

PRECOGNITION
'No! No – don't...'

As John Williams watched, a distinguished-looking man in a blue coat and white waistcoat entered the lobby of the House of Commons, flanked by Members of Parliament. He was none other than Spencer Perceval, the British Prime Minister. Moments later, Williams saw another man enter the lobby, dressed in a brown coat with gold buttons. To Williams' horror, the man drew out a small pistol and fired it straight at the Prime Minister, who fell to the ground as blood spread across his waistcoat. Immediately several men grabbed hold of the murderer…

At that moment, Williams sat up in bed in horror, sweat glistening on his face. Waking his wife, he told her what had happened but she reassured him that he'd had a bad dream. Still feeling uneasy, Williams went back to sleep, only to have exactly the same dream again. Once again his wife reassured him when he woke up but, having fallen asleep a second time, the dream was again repeated.

Next day, Williams was haunted by his dream and wondered what he should do. Should he leave his home in Cornwall and travel to London to warn the Prime Minister, or would he just be branded a madman? Surely no one would take him seriously. Having discussed the matter with several friends in town, he decided to stay at home, but he scanned the newspapers anxiously for any news from the Houses of Parliament in Westminster.

A week or so later, on 11 May 1812, Spencer Perceval left 10 Downing Street and, because it was such a fine day, decided he would walk to the House.

At around 5.15pm, Perceval entered the lobby of the Houses of Parliament. Just seconds later, a man called John Bellingham, dressed in a brown coat with gold buttons, stepped out from behind a pillar, drew a pistol from his clothes and…

LIFT THE FLAP
TO FIND OUT MORE

GLOSSARY

Abduction When a person is taken by force.

Archaeologist A person who studies ancient places and objects.

Assassination When an important political person is murdered.

Brigantine A two-masted sailing ship.

Conquistador The Spanish word for conqueror. The conquistadors were the Spanish soldiers who invaded Central and South America in the 16th century.

Hominid An early human being.

Hydrophones Instruments that convert sound travelling through water into electrical signals.

Lenticular Shaped like a curved lens.

Meteorite A rock-like object from space that enters the Earth's atmosphere.

Paranormal Something that cannot be explained normally.

Plesiosaur A long-necked prehistoric sea reptile.

Surveillance Surveillance equipment is used to keep a person or a group of people under observation.

INDEX

CONTENTS

The World's Water

Most people in the developed world never give a thought to water. It is there when we turn on the tap. We can buy bottled water at every supermarket and café. We wash in it, swim in it and flush away our waste with it. Yet it is one of the most precious resources we have.

Two fifths of the world's population are short of water already, and the problem is going to get worse quickly. Within 25 years, between half and two-thirds of the people in the world will be suffering from a severe shortage of water. How did this happen – and what can we do about it?

Why we need water

People need fresh, clean water. We all need water to drink, to wash ourselves and our clothes, to cook with and to wash food. Industry and farming use even more water. Our need for water is growing all the time, but the amount of water available for each person is shrinking.

Water shortages lead to misery, disease and death. Half of the people who are ill in the world at any one time are suffering from diseases carried by unclean water. Crops will not grow without water, leading to famine and starvation. When people are desperately short of water, they take it from wherever they can. This may cause conflicts and wars.

FACE THE **FACTS**

Of the fresh water used in the world each year, only 8 per cent goes on domestic use – drinking, cooking and washing. A large slice – 22 per cent – is used by industry. Around 70 per cent is used by farmers watering crops and raising animals. The total amount of water we use is increasing all the time.

A finite resource

There is a fixed amount of water on earth. Scientists calculate that it is 1.4 billion cubic kilometres. It sounds like a lot, but less than 3 per cent of it is fresh water. The rest is sea water. Much of the fresh water is locked away in places where we cannot use it – in the polar ice caps or deep underground. Just 0.77 per cent of the total water on earth is available for use by people. The water most easily accessible to humans is that which falls as rain and snow each year, and it comes to only 34,000 cubic kilometres. If we could force that water into a cube, each side would be just 32.5 km long.

A farmer in Mali collects water from a water hole to irrigate his onion crop in the dry season.

The water cycle

Water constantly cycles through different states. It falls as rain or snow on to the land and sea. If it falls on the land, it may soak into the ground, evaporate again, or run off into streams and rivers. Some of the water that sinks into the ground is taken up by plants and trees and released back into the atmosphere. Some collects underground in aquifers. Groundwater rises again from aquifers to form springs which run into rivers. Water also flows slowly underground to the sea.

Some rain and snow falls over high mountains and freezes in glaciers. Glaciers slowly flow downhill, and each year part of a glacier melts and feeds streams and rivers. River water flows to the sea.

Water evaporates from both the land and the sea. This water vapour rises and cools, then collects in clouds as water droplets. The droplets eventually fall again as rain, snow, sleet or hail. This complex path of water through the atmosphere, land and oceans is called the water cycle.

The water cycle. There is no new water on earth. This means we are drinking the same water that the dinosaurs drank!

The water cycle

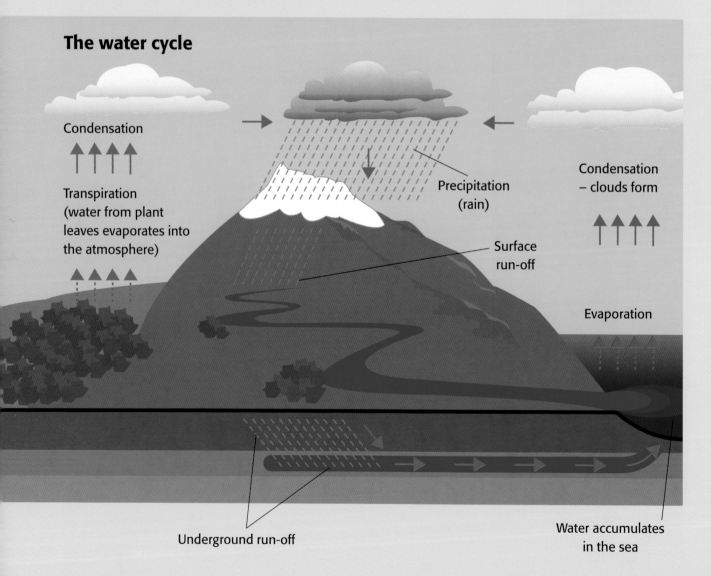

Condensation

Transpiration
(water from plant
leaves evaporates into
the atmosphere)

Precipitation
(rain)

Surface
run-off

Condensation
– clouds form

Evaporation

Underground run-off

Water accumulates
in the sea

Moraine Lake in Canada is formed from melting glacier water. It is at its fullest in June.

The role of vegetation

For the last 500 million years, plants and trees have played an important role in the water cycle. They take up water from the soil and release it into the atmosphere during respiration. Water that falls on to leaves reaches the ground more slowly than water falling on to bare soil or rock. It drips and runs to the ground, giving time for water to soak away into aquifers. Some water evaporates directly from the leaves.

The roots of plants help to hold the soil in place and stop it washing away when run-off water pours over the land. Where land has been cleared, the soil quickly washes away. The run-off then washes straight into rivers, and very little seeps into the ground.

FACE THE **FACTS**

As more and more land is built on or paved, there are fewer areas of open soil where water can soak away and replenish aquifers. Instead, the water runs over the surface and into drains. In times of heavy rain, drains are over-filled and rivers burst their banks, causing flooding.

9

This young girl in a remote village in Laos, in south-east Asia, has to collect water from a standpipe. The villagers do not have running water in their homes.

Where does our water come from?

Throughout history, people have used water as it moves through the water cycle by collecting rainwater, taking water from rivers, and digging wells. We still use all these methods, but nowadays people are taking more and more water and are looking for new sources of fresh water. We pump water from underground, emptying ancient aquifers. In some places, people use sea water, first removing the salt from it. Also, rivers are diverted or dammed along their length so that in some places very little is left to run into the sea.

Water underground

Scientists distinguish between two types of underground water. Meteoric water is part of the water cycle. It feeds springs and is replaced by rainfall. Fossil water has been stored underground for a very long time. It is cut off from the water cycle, often lying deep within impermeable rock in aquifers. Aquifers play an essential role in the water cycle and in the balance of life on earth. Yet all over the world, people are draining aquifers more quickly than rainfall can replenish them, with catastrophic results. By taking fossil water, we are draining water supplies that will not renew themselves.

Facing the challenge

One of the Millennium Development Goals set by the United Nations (UN) in 2000 is to halve the number of people without access to clean water by 2015. This is a massive challenge. We must share water more fairly and become responsible custodians of the world's water, using and preserving water more carefully. We must stop draining underground sources and emptying rivers. We must tackle climate change and its effects on the supply of water, and we must make sure the changes we make are sustainable and do not set up problems for future generations. It will take massive political, social and technological change over the coming years.

FACE THE **FACTS**

The average European uses 200 litres of water every day. The average person in the developing world uses 10 litres of water for drinking, washing and cooking. If we continue to use water as we do now, in 20 years' time humans will use 40 per cent more water than they do now.

CHAPTER 1

Water in the Past

As soon as humans began farming, more than 13,000 years ago, they needed water to irrigate crops. Early settlements often sprang up near rivers, where water was readily available.

Ancient systems of water management

People all around the world came up with similar solutions to the problems of water supply. They built dams, reservoirs and canals to control and divert rivers.

Farmers ploughing a field in an ancient Egyptian fresco. The River Nile flooded regularly, and Egyptian farmers used the floodwater to irrigate their crops.

A dam is a barrier built across a river to slow or stop its flow. A reservoir is a large body of stored water, often collected by damming or diverting a river. A canal is an artificially constructed channel for water. The earliest known irrigation canals were made in Mesopotamia (present-day Iraq) 6,000 years ago.

In many places, farmers depended on regular floods to fill reservoirs or pools. The ancient Egyptians harnessed the floods of the River Nile, and in North America the Anasazi people diverted flood and river waters to their fields through canals. People worldwide dug wells, built terraced fields with stone walls to catch run-off and hold it in pools, and used layers of stones to trap water so that it would seep into the ground.

Master builders

The Sinhalese people of Sri Lanka had the most advanced irrigation system of the ancient world. More recently – around 1,500 years ago – their knowledge of hydraulic engineering enabled them to cultivate land that would otherwise have been too dry. They were able to supply cities with water from distant rivers and reservoirs. The Sinhalese built vast tanks, dug canals many kilometres long and developed an early version of the sluice gates used to control modern dams.

Water in cities

Most cities originally took their water from rivers and wells, but later laid water pipes. Urban water supplies were easily polluted with sewage and industrial waste. In nineteenth-century Europe, thousands of people died in epidemics of deadly diseases such as typhoid and cholera until good sewerage systems separated foul water and drinking water.

A well-head in the courtyard of Casa Goldoni in Venice, Italy. The well provided fresh water for the people living in the house.

SUSTAINABLE TECHNOLOGIES

Venice

The Italian city of Venice is built on a series of islands in the sea. It has no access to rivers. From the Middle Ages until the late twentieth century, all rainwater falling on to buildings and paving was caught by drains and directed to underground stores beneath the courtyards. The water was filtered through layers of stones and sand, and fed a well located in the centre of each courtyard.

Into the modern era

Traditional methods of digging wells, building canals and drawing water from rivers supplied sufficient water for thousands of years. Yet over the last fifty years, these methods have not provided enough water for a growing population with increasingly water-hungry lifestyles. We have employed technology to draw water from the earth's supplies ever faster.

Water from under our feet

A traditional well fills naturally. It is dug into the water table, and water flows in from saturated (soaking wet) ground or an underground stream. Modern wells can take much more water and can be extremely damaging. They are up to 900 m deep and pump water from underground, effectively sucking it from aquifers. When water is pumped out of the ground faster than the aquifer can refill, the process is called water mining.

In many places, so much water has been pumped from deep underground that other wells have dried up, leaving farmers and villagers with no water supply. Eventually, a mined aquifer will dry up, and the land above will become unstable. Parts of Mexico City are already subsiding into emptying aquifers at the rate of 50 cm a year.

FACE THE **FACTS**

The Ogallala aquifer in the USA is the largest underground water supply, originally containing an estimated 4 trillion tonnes of water. This fossil water is being depleted fourteen times as fast as it can refill. The Ogallala supplies water for one-fifth of the irrigated land in the USA. Half of it may have been used up already.

This cotton field in Texas, USA, is irrigated with water from the Ogallala aquifer. Cotton is a crop that needs a large amount of water to grow.

The Hoover Dam on the Colorado River, on the border between Nevada and Arizona. At just over 220 m high, it is the second largest dam in the USA.

Water from rivers

All methods that take water from a river reduce its flow. There are so many interventions in some rivers that no water, or only a tiny trickle, reaches the sea. There are now 500,000 large dams worldwide. Dams can help to regulate the flow of rivers, preventing extreme and disastrous flooding. They are also built to provide hydroelectric power (see page 18). This type of technology has succeeded in providing water for people upstream – but at the expense of people and wildlife downstream.

CHAPTER 2

Pressures on Water Resources

Pressures on water have increased very quickly. The world's population is growing, and we are using more and more water. The effects of climate change are also having an impact on the availability of water, and efforts to extract water in the recent past are now affecting the supply.

More people using more water

The world's population is growing rapidly, particularly in areas that are already short of water. In September 2008, the world population was around 6.7 billion, and is expected to rise to 9 billion by 2042. All these people will need water. Not only are there more people, but also we are each using more water. As people in China and India become wealthier, they install showers and flush toilets. Industrial processes use even greater amounts of water. The demand for crops to feed the increasing population is also rising. A growing number of people around the world expect to eat meat, which takes far more water to produce than plant-based foods.

Cattle on a farm in Xinjiang Uygur Autonomous Region, China. Farming animals for meat takes a lot of water, yet it is on the increase.

In the right place, at the right time

Long ago, civilizations grew up where water was available. Today, we have huge cities that cannot possibly be sustained by local water supplies alone. We farm dry areas, often growing crops that require a lot of water.

Water is unevenly distributed over the earth, and often it is not where we really need it to be. For example, China is home to a quarter of the world's people, yet it has only 6 per cent of the world's supply of fresh water. Now we have the technologies to move water to where people are living – but often this has disastrous consequences.

This map shows the water footprint of different countries. A country's water footprint is the amount of fresh water used to produce the goods and services that it consumes. The green areas are places where the nation's water footprint is equal to or smaller than the global average. Countries in red have a water footprint above world average.

FACE THE **FACTS**

The World Health Organization (WHO) considers 'reasonable access to water' to be not less than 20 litres per person per day, or 7,300 litres a year. The average domestic water use in Canada is 292,000 litres a year, while in the eastern African nation of Djibouti it is only 1,000 litres a year.

Average national water footprint
(cubic metres per person per year)

- 600–800
- 800–1000
- 1000–1200
- 1200–1300
- 1300–1500
- 1500–1800
- 1800–2100
- 2100–2500
- No data

Source: Water Footprint Network, 2008

Tapping the source

In many areas people have diverted rivers and drained water from underground to such a degree that their neighbours have no water left. Rivers that are diverted or depleted along their course to the sea may have too little flow to be useful to people who live downstream. For example, in 2001 the Rio Grande in North America did not reach the Gulf of Mexico because there was no water left in it by the time it reached the coast. Where a lot of water is pumped from underground, the water table drops and shallower wells, which once served people's needs, dry up completely. The usual pattern is that large farms, industrial corporations or towns and cities draw off the water they need and little or none is left for rural areas and small farmers.

Water for power

Water from rivers is also used to produce power. Hydroelectric power stations depend on the flow of water to generate electricity. If too much water is drawn from a river upstream, there may not be enough force in the river's flow to generate power. Hydroelectric power stations also have an impact on river users downstream because they harness and control the river's flow, often using dams and sluices to regulate it.

The Hoa Binh hydroelectric power station near Hanoi, in North Vietnam. Built on the Da River, it is the largest hydroelectric power station in the country.

Making people pay

Water clearly has great importance for industry, farming and the supply of electricity. Since the 1980s, many governments have decided that people should pay more money for water. They are keen to involve private water companies in building a modern, efficient system and managing the supply of water. International organizations such as the World Bank and International Monetary Fund have also encouraged the privatization of water supplies. This has led to large international corporations controlling water all over the world. The French companies Suez-ONDEO and Vivendi-Veolia control over 70 per cent of the world water market between them.

While some people think treating water as a commodity will encourage people to value this resource and use it sparingly, others believe water is a basic human right that should be available to everyone, whether they are rich or poor.

Women in Dar es Salaam, Tanzania, buy water from a water seller at high prices. The World Bank funded the privatization of water in the city, but the private company failed to mend broken pipes, and water quality declined. In 2005 the Tanzanian government cancelled the contract.

PERSPECTIVE

Rights to water

'While the private sector can help in some areas, the poorest of the poor need revitalised and reformed public systems which do not emphasise profits, but instead focus on enhancing poor people's entitlements and rights to water.'

Dr Lyla Mehta, Institute of Development Studies, University of Sussex, UK

Climate change and water

It is not only water policies that are affecting supply. Our climate is changing, and the earth is warming up. Global warming is having an effect on the distribution of fresh water, and climate change is affecting where and when rain falls. Some places are becoming hotter and drier while others are becoming wetter and more prone to flooding. Farmers have to adapt to these changing weather patterns. As change continues, some will have to grow different crops, better suited to the new climate in their area. Others will find that their land can no longer produce enough food for them to make a living.

Shrinking glaciers

The effects of climate change on glaciers will also have a devastating effect on water supply. Glaciers are frozen rivers in high mountains and the polar regions. They contain vast expanses of fresh water locked away in ice. In springtime, glaciers begin to melt and the water flows down the mountains, feeding streams and rivers. In the winter, more snow falls and the glaciers build up again.

Glaciers in the Andes, such as this one in Peru, provide essential water to local people as they melt in the spring and feed lakes, rivers and streams.

These Sherpa women in the Himalayas are sitting in an area that used to be covered with snow all winter, but now has less and less snow. Glaciers are shrinking throughout the Himalayas.

In many parts of the world, people rely on the melt water from glaciers for their water supply. Yet over the last twenty to thirty years, the glaciers have been shrinking rapidly. The summer is hotter and comes earlier, so more ice melts, but the winter is warmer too and there is less snowfall. The glaciers do not have time to build up again before the next spring comes. They are disappearing – and with them, the water supply for hundreds of millions of people. For example, the glaciers of the Himalayas provide water for a billion people in India, Pakistan, Tibet and China. One of the largest, the Parbati glacier, retreated an average of 52 m a year during the 1990s. When the glaciers melt, this will first cause devastating flooding and then lead to major rivers drying up.

PERSPECTIVE

Preserving our water

'The temperature of the earth is rising. It is not natural. The Sherpas of Khumbu [in Nepal] may not know everything, but they are suffering the consequences of the people's greed. We mountain people should be careful and take precautions. If we don't save Khumbu today our fresh water will dry up and the problem will be impossible to solve in the future.'

Ngawang Tenzing Jangpo, Abbot of Tengboche monastery, Khumbu, Nepal

Falling ice, rising seas

Another effect of global warming is that the polar ice sheets are melting. As the ice melts, water pours into the sea, raising sea levels around the world. The fresh water of the ice is lost in the ocean, depleting the world's stock of fresh water for ever.

Rising sea levels cause flooding in low-lying areas around the world. Sea water flows up rivers and pollutes estuaries and deltas with salt. Once the ground has a high salt content, crops will no longer grow there. Salt seeps into the water table and pollutes wells.

Rain and wind

The changing climate does not just mean that many places are hotter. Patterns of rainfall and wind are dependent on air temperature. Some areas will see much less rainfall and experience droughts, while other areas will have more intense rainfall and flooding. Hot air over the sea will lead to more tropical storms. These have a devastating effect when they hit land, causing flooding and widespread destruction. With changing rainfall and the disappearance of glaciers, the seasonal swelling and flooding of rivers also changes. This will affect people who farm flood plains and depend on established patterns of seasonal flooding.

Fewer trees, less rain

Trees also play an important role in the water cycle. In many areas of the world, people have cut down forests to clear ground for farming and building. Removing them reduces the amount of water that can be recycled from the ground (see page 9). Water vapour released into the air by trees condenses to form clouds locally, which falls again as rain. Yet if water runs off and collects in rivers, it is carried away before it can evaporate and form rain clouds.

This land in Brazil once formed part of the Atlantic Forest, a lush rain forest. By 2007, only 10 per cent of the forest remained.

Dirty water

More and more of the water returning to the rivers, seas and earth is dirty. It is polluted with human and animal waste, with heavy metals and organic pollutants from industry, and with fertilizers and pesticides from farming. Water treatment removes harmful bacteria, but many other pollutants remain. Waste dumped in or on the ground also contains chemicals that are washed down into aquifers, polluting the groundwater. Rapid industrialization in India, China and parts of Africa has led to many aquifers becoming polluted.

A man wades through floodwater on one of the nine low-lying islands of Tuvalu, in the South Pacific. Tuvalu is likely to be the first country lost to rising sea levels, bringing disaster to the 10,000 people who live there.

FACE THE **FACTS**

In the USA, 40 per cent of the streams and rivers are so polluted that they are considered too dangerous for swimming, fishing or drinking.

CHAPTER 3

The Human Dimension

The lack of a reliable clean water supply can be deadly for the 1.1 billion people who live with water scarcity. It affects people in many areas of the world, and not just in less economically developed regions.

Water for sale

When water becomes a commodity, the people who have least money are most likely to suffer. Water is taken from rivers and aquifers to supply paying customers, leaving little or none for people who have traditionally taken water directly from rivers and wells. If they cannot afford to be connected to a mains water supply, they may have to travel long distances to collect water, or buy water from travelling water sellers who charge high prices. People become very vulnerable – sometimes they cannot afford water, and sometimes none is available.

Even in cities with a modern water supply and drainage system, people who cannot pay for water may have their supply cut off. In some regions of the USA, there are thousands of people who have lost their access to water because they are unable to pay their water bills.

Demonstrators in Detroit, USA, in 2003 protest about the withdrawal of water supplies to people who cannot pay for water.

They have to beg water from people who still have a supply. Some desperate people pay for an illegal reconnection, tapping in to the mains supply without paying for the water they are taking. As water becomes increasingly scarce and expensive, more and more people will be put in the position of living with too little water in the midst of people who have plenty.

Long walks

In many parts of the world, people have to walk to collect water each day. As rivers and wells dry up, they have to walk further and further. Sometimes they arrive at the pump or well and find there is no water. In Africa and Asia, women walk an average of six kilometres to collect water, and carry 20 kg of water home.

PERSPECTIVE

Fighting for water

'We indigenous peoples wish to live and to breathe the Xingu River. Its water is the source of life and we don't want to die. We will not give up on life and we will not abandon our struggle. Our war cries are surging in our throats to oppose the enemy.'

Official statement by indigenous (native) peoples who depend on the Xingu River, Brazil. Their water supply is threatened by the proposed damming of the river.

Two girls returning to their village with water collected from a well in Rajasthan, India. Rajasthan is one of the driest states in India.

Famine

Changing rainfall patterns, falling water tables and shrinking rivers mean that farmers in many areas are finding it increasingly difficult to water their crops. Famine and starvation can quickly follow if harvests fail. Those people who cannot afford to buy food from other areas will have nothing to eat.

Expanding deserts

Desertification is the process of land becoming desert. In long periods of hot, dry weather, vegetation dies and the soil dries out. The loss of plants means that topsoil can easily blow away. Once it is gone, the land is no longer usable for farming.

Forced to move

When farmland is lost, people have to move, seeking somewhere to live where they will have a water supply and be able to grow crops. The influx of displaced people into other areas can easily lead to conflict. It puts increased pressure on the supply of water and food in those regions. It may lead to open hostility and even war.

Wars for water

War in the Darfur region of Sudan in northern Africa has been caused in part by the displacement of nomadic people who have been driven from their land by lack of water. They have moved south to areas occupied by farmers, who are protective of their land and its water supply.

There is potential for further conflict over water. Most of the world's major rivers run through more than one country, and 90 per cent of the world's population live in areas where the water supply is shared with other countries. Where communities and industries in the upstream country draw water from the river, they reduce the flow for people living in the country downstream. Political tension over this vital resource can mount quickly.

Aquifers may also span more than country and supply water to people over a large area. They can be a source of tension if people in one region think others are drawing more than their fair share.

(opposite) These refugees, studying at an outdoor primary school, are victims of the conflict in Darfur, Sudan. Having fled their homes, they are staying in Bredjing refugee camp in eastern Chad.

FACE THE **FACTS**

The English word 'rival' is from the Latin *rivalis*, which means 'one using the same river as another.' There are 263 rivers, aquifers and other water sources shared between two or more countries. In the 50 years from 1956 to 2006, there were 37 international conflicts over water, 30 of them in the Middle East.

This power and water desalination plant in Kuwait was destroyed by Iraqi forces during the Gulf War in 1990–91.

Water as a weapon

There is a long history of water being used as a weapon of war and these conflicts continue today. In 1967, Israel took control of the River Jordan and still will not allow Palestinians in the Israeli-occupied West Bank to sink boreholes without permission. Israel also disputed the building of pipes and pumps by Lebanon to draw water from the Wazzani River, which flows into Israel from the north. The water, taken 5 km north of the Israeli border, reduces the flow available to people living in Israel.

Clean and dirty water

The effects of dirty water can be as bad as having no water. Water may be polluted with harmful micro-organisms, parasites, chemical pollutants and even prescription drugs which pass through people and are carried into rivers and aquifers. Stagnant water attracts dangerous insects, such as malaria-carrying mosquitoes. Dirty water kills ten times as many people in the world each year as wars and conflicts.

In many parts of the world, human and animal waste flows straight into streams, rivers or the sea, or is left on land where it can pollute underground water sources or be carried into waterways. It is not just a problem of the developing world. In 1995, half of the people living in southern Europe did not have a connection to mains sewerage.

PERSPECTIVE

Child deaths

At least 10 per cent of child mortality here is because of the water. And of the remainder, at least 90 per cent of deaths are related to water. . . . [Parents] just don't have water to wash the clothes. . . . They don't have water to bathe the child every day.'

Community doctor, Bolivia

Not just us

The world's fresh water is a resource not only for human beings but also for all of nature. As we squander and pollute this resource, we destroy the habitats needed by plants and animals. Many species are being driven out of areas they once inhabited, and some are disappearing completely. We have a responsibility to protect other species from harm resulting from our activities. Reduced biodiversity will have an impact on people, too. Life on earth forms a complex web, with species depending on one another – disruption can have far-reaching consequences.

A bird in Rajasthan, India, stands in heavily polluted water. Dirty water is a danger to wildlife and people.

CHAPTER 4

Technological Solutions

Technology can help to provide the world with clean water and process waste water. Yet some of the technological solutions of the past have made the problem worse. Sustainable solutions are needed that do not contribute to climate change.

New water for old

Much of the water we use returns to nature in a dirty state. The polluted water is dangerous to human health and damaging to wildlife, so it must be cleaned if our use of water is to be sustainable. This could be done using technologies already available. Used water that is not excessively dirty – water from baths, cooking and washing clothes, for example – is called grey water. Sometimes it can be reused without processing; it may be used to flush toilets or water gardens.

In industrialized countries, water that is flushed down the drains goes to sewage treatment plants. Water from industrial processes can be captured, cleaned and recycled, too, though some pollutants must be removed by chemical reactions. In some places, water is cleaned in this way before it is returned to nature. In other areas, more money must be invested in the equipment needed to make sure water is properly cleaned.

A worker at a sewage treatment plant in Sydney, Australia, draws off a sample of reclaimed water.

SUSTAINABLE TECHNOLOGIES

Treating waste water

Waste water collected at a sewage treatment plant is processed in several stages. First, solid waste is removed. Floating waste is raked off the top of the water and sinking waste, such as stones and sand, is allowed to settle out. Next, grease is skimmed from the top, and sediment is allowed to fall to the bottom. Next, micro-organisms are used to break down biological waste. Biological material called floc collects and is filtered from the water. Finally, chemical by-products of the biological processes are removed, and the water is disinfected.

Desalination

Desalination means removing salt from water to make fresh water. It is used to process sea water so that it can be used for drinking and irrigation. Ships and submarines have used desalinated water for many years. Now, some coastal areas are building large desalination plants to produce water for whole towns and cities. The largest is the Jebel Ali plant in the United Arab Emirates. It produces 300 million cubic metres of water a year, or 9,500 litres a second – nearly ten times as much as the largest desalination plant in the USA. By the beginning of 2008, there were 13,080 desalination plants around the world, producing more than 55 billion litres of water a day.

Kuwait is a desert country with very little rainfall. This desalination plant in Doha, Kuwait, supplies all the drinking water for people living in the area.

Problems with desalination

Many desalination plants are in the Middle East, where oil to run them is cheap and plentiful. However, oil-fired plants produce large amounts of carbon emissions. These contribute to the build-up of greenhouse gases, which is causing climate change.

Desalination plants produce salt as a by-product. This must be removed to a place where it cannot enter the water table or rivers. Many scientists believe that the salt and carbon emissions produced by most desalination plants outweigh the benefits of the fresh water produced.

Desalination for the future

Conventional desalination plants either boil water at low pressure, using distillation to produce fresh water, or force water through a membrane. Salt cannot pass through the membrane and is left behind. This uses less energy than distillation.

A new type of membrane was announced in 2008 that should make the desalination process six or seven times more efficient. Desalination would require less energy and could be powered by solar panels or wind energy to produce fresh water without carbon emissions. A desalination plant in Perth, Australia, is already partly powered by wind energy, and a new plant planned for Sydney will be powered entirely by renewable energy.

Fog harvesting

Fog consists of droplets of water suspended in the air. It can be collected to supply fresh water. The first full-scale fog harvesting system was built in the fishing village of Chungungo, Chile, in 1987. Chungungo had previously relied on water delivered by truck. After the fog harvesting system was introduced, the village was able to provide its own drinking water and had enough to spare to begin growing crops for sale.

Fog harvesting produces a good yield only in areas where the wind direction is predictable and there is a raised area on which the system can be built. There must be a predictable foggy period. High coastal dunes or hills, and some mountain areas with low-lying cloud, are good for fog harvesting. In some places, fog is seasonal so the water is not available all year.

(opposite) A woman carries water harvested from fog near the Indian border in Megma, Nepal. The fog harvesting system has provided sufficient water for a school in the village.

SUSTAINABLE TECHNOLOGIES

The fog harvesting system

A fog harvesting system is made from layers of nylon net stretched across a frame set across the wind. The water in the fog condenses on the netting and trickles down to a collecting trough at the base of the net. Gravity carries the water along the trough to collect in a tank. In some places, water can also be delivered to the point of use by gravity. Up to 30 per cent of the water carried in the fog can be harvested.

Chewang Norphel, director of the Leh Nutrition Project in Tibet, shows a water channel that diverts water to make an artificial glacier close to a village near Leh, Ladakh.

Artificial glaciers

Ladakh is a region in the Himalayas between Pakistan and China. It has only 7 cm of rainfall a year. Glaciers are a crucial source of water for farmers in Ladakh, but often the melt waters come too late to irrigate crops. Artificial glaciers are now providing a new source of water. Using a system of pipes, water from a stream is directed to a shady valley and from there flows over a sloping hillside. Low stone embankments stop the water, forcing it to collect in shallow pools. In winter, the pools freeze to make a long, shallow glacier. This melts before the taller glaciers, giving the farmers water at the start of the growing season. The largest artificial glacier built so far is 300 m long, 45 m wide and 1 m deep. It supplies all the water for a village of 700 people. Because the technology is simple, artificial glaciers can be built by local people from cheap components.

Seeding clouds

Rains that do not come when expected often cost farmers their crops and can cause famine. One way of dealing with it is to 'seed' rainclouds, forcing rain to fall. Cloud seeding is widely used in China because of water shortages. It is used to encourage rain to fall in dry areas to prevent drought.

It is difficult to control the rainfall though, so some areas may receive more than others. This can lead to disputes if people believe 'their' rain has been hijacked and forced to fall elsewhere. Scientists are uncertain whether cloud seeding actually produces more rain or just moves rain from one place to another. In either case, it can make rain fall where farmers need it, but must be used carefully to avoid disadvantaging one region to help another.

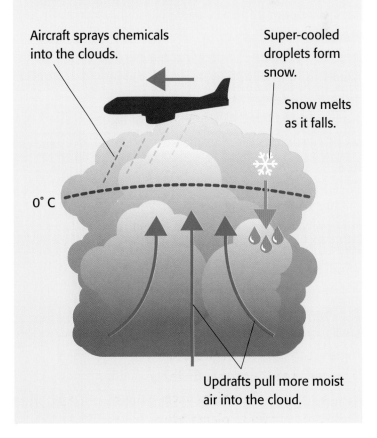

SUSTAINABLE TECHNOLOGIES

Cloud seeding

Aircraft or ground-launched rockets fire crystals of silver iodide or dry ice (solid carbon dioxide) into a cloud. The seeding causes tiny water droplets to cluster together into large drops. These freeze into snow then fall, melting as they travel through warmer air. More moist air is pulled up into the cloud, so the cloud reforms.

Aircraft sprays chemicals into the clouds.

Super-cooled droplets form snow.

Snow melts as it falls.

0° C

Updrafts pull more moist air into the cloud.

CHAPTER 5

Saving for a Secure Future

The world has enough water to supply all our needs if we use it carefully, but it is wasted in many ways. It is also dirtied and released without cleaning, used inefficiently and exploited unfairly. We must all learn to use water more efficiently, and to adjust our expectations.

Irrigation

Irrigation is especially important in areas that are dry or have long, dry spells and then a rainy season. Irrigated land is much more productive than unirrigated land; 40 per cent of the world's food comes from irrigated land. As some areas of the world become even drier, with less rainfall and a falling water table, they will rely increasingly on irrigation.

There are problems with irrigation, though. When land is irrigated, it is more heavily tilled. This breaks up the soil into smaller particles that are more easily displaced. Whenever the soil is dry, it is readily blown away, leading to parched, sterile land. All water contains dissolved mineral salts of several types. If land is over-irrigated without proper drainage, salts build up in the soil. In high concentrations, these are harmful to plants. When water

These soya-bean fields in Brazil are irrigated using conventional methods, which involve spraying water on to the plants from above.

evaporates or is taken up by plants, the salts are left behind. As more and more water is used, the deposits of salts increase until the soil is no longer usable for farming. Salt build-up affects around one-fifth of the world's farmland and causes one million hectares of land to be abandoned each year.

Drip irrigation

Conventional modern irrigation uses a lot of water. Since the 1930s, the most common form of irrigation has involved spraying vast areas with water from sprinklers. Much of the water is wasted; either it evaporates or it never reaches the roots of crops. New methods of drip irrigation use less water and are just as good (or better) at increasing crop yields. Yet in 2008, less than 1 per cent of the world's irrigated land used drip irrigation methods.

This diagram shows drip irrigation. A water tank in the village catches the rain and stores it so that farmers can use it for irrigating their crops.

SUSTAINABLE TECHNOLOGIES

How drip irrigation works

Rainwater is collected in a large tank. The farmer stands a bucket of water on a platform near the crops, with long hoses running from the bottom of the bucket alongside the rows of plants. Small holes in the hose allow a trickle of water to each plant. Gravity pulls the water down into the hose; as the water seeps into the soil, more water flows along the hose. It takes only 30 m of pipe to water 100–200 plants.

Farmer fills a 20-litre drip bucket and places it 1 m above the ground on poles.

Gravity forces the water through the hose.

Bucket is attached to a long hose that crosses the crop field.

Water drips through the holes in the hose on to the plant roots.

1 m

Using a system of pipes, taps and valves, water is delivered at a slow but steady rate directly to plants. The drier the soil, the more slowly the water is released, to avoid loss through deep drainage and evaporation. The technique is ancient – thousands of years ago, people in many areas filled clay pots with water and buried them underground near crops. The water slowly leaked through the pot to feed the roots.

Because a drip irrigation system delivers water straight to the ground, recycled and waste water can be used. (Water containing detergents or other substances is not sprayed directly on to the plants, but can be used for drip irrigation.) Sometimes fertilizers are added directly to the water. The targeted delivery means much less fertilizer is used – sometimes only 5 per cent of the amount required previously.

(opposite) Tropical sugar beet going to be processed in India. This crop requires little water to grow, and may be used to produce sugar or as a biofuel.

Growing suitable crops

It may seem obvious that areas with less water should grow crops that need little watering. In many dry areas, farmers have made money from growing luxury crops for export, but these often take a lot of water to grow. For example, in some African countries, such as Kenya and Zimbabwe, fresh vegetables and flowers are grown for sale to developed countries. As water becomes scarcer, some farmers are beginning to switch to crops better suited to their local conditions. In parts of India, farmers have been encouraged to replace sugar cane with sugar beet, a crop which requires less water. These farmers have to buy new equipment and adapt to new methods of farming.

Rainwater harvesting

Many parts of the world have uneven rainfall during the year; there are dry periods and wet periods. This can create difficult conditions for farmers, since rain may not fall at the times their crops need most water. In some places, people use rainwater harvesting to collect rain when it falls and store it in tanks for dry times. Rainwater harvesting can even replenish drying aquifers.

The village of Tilonia in Rajasthan, India, has 15–40 cm of rain each year, which all falls in the rainy season (July to September). A network of pipes and drains takes the water into pits from which it sinks into the ground and eventually feeds wells. Even in the driest years, the villagers do not run out of water.

PERSPECTIVE

Harvesting rainwater in India

'In an 80,000 square feet area we can collect 700,000 litres of water for as little as 100 millimetres of rain. It's a traditional solution using local skills and knowledge and tapping the resources of the local community.'

Lakshman Singh, environmentalist in Rajasthan, India

Cutting waste

When water supplies are piped over long distances or through cities, water is often lost through leaks. In parts of South America, more than 50 per cent of water in cities and up to 75 per cent of water for irrigation leaks away. One benefit claimed for privatizing water supplies is that large corporations can afford to repair and replace old pipes and pumps, cutting waste.

Using new technology, water supply companies can monitor the pipes. Sensors buried underground with pipes detect leaks as soon as they happen and send an alert to a computer system. Engineers then quickly make repairs.

These workers in London, England, are repairing water pipes that are nearly 150 years old. Old pipes like these are particularly prone to leaks.

Saving water at home

More efficient use of water at home can also make a big difference to the total water we use. A dripping tap can waste more than 5,000 litres of water a year, so keeping plumbing in good repair is important. People can use a dual flush toilet, put a water-saving device in the cistern, and have a quick shower instead of a deep bath. Aerated taps and showers mix water with air and use half the water of conventional taps. Using a dishwasher or washing machine only when it is full also cuts domestic water use. Newer models use less water than old models. A type of washing machine invented in 2008 uses a single cup of water to clean a full load of washing.

Legislating for careful water use

Governments can help by passing laws that require industries to clean their water. In Suzhou City, China, new and extended factories must recycle at least 50 per cent of their waste water. In Los Angeles, USA, measures announced in 2008 will include porous paving in parking lots so that water can run through into the ground, waterless urinals in public buildings, rules to limit people washing cars and watering lawns, and a plan to clean waste water.

SUSTAINABLE TECHNOLOGIES

Space toilets

New toilets of Russian design in the International Space Station clean human waste to a sufficiently high degree that the water can be reused for drinking. The space station is a closed environment, with infrequent deliveries of fresh water, so it is important to maintain an efficient water cycle, reusing the same water repeatedly. The toilet system works by repeatedly filtering waste to remove all non-water molecules.

Unless industrial processes are designed to clean and recycle water, they use vast quantities, and return it to rivers in a dirty state. This car factory in Guangzhou, China, which opened in 2006, incorporates state-of-the-art technology. The plant also recycles all its water.

CHAPTER 6

A Fairer World

While the richest people in developed nations enjoy lush gardens, watered golf courses and swimming pools, others do not have enough safe water to live on. A fairer distribution of the world's resources will take political change and cooperation.

Sharing water

In many places, rivers and aquifers supply more than one country (see page 26), but the water need not be a source of conflict. Some countries have negotiated fair use of water. Since 1960, despite other conflicts between the two countries, India and Pakistan have managed the waters of the Indus River jointly through the Indus Waters Treaty. Many nations have seen that cooperation in managing water is preferable to wars over water. While some people fear wars over water, others are hopeful that more international agreements and treaties can be forged.

Following the protests in 2000, the people of Bolivia won the right to water they could afford.

Treating water as a right

Some countries have torn up agreements with international water corporations because privatizing the water supply caused problems for poorer people. In other places, people themselves have taken action against water corporations. Cochabamba is a desert region of Bolivia. In 1999, the water supply was privatized, passing to the international business Bechtel. Water bills rose to prices local people could not afford. At the start of 2000, citizens formed The Coalition in Defence of Water and Life and began protests and strikes. Hostility between Bechtel and the protesters increased, with rioting and legal actions. In April 2000, the water supply was nationalized again, and water rates returned to their previous level.

Children queue to collect water from a well in Uganda. The water in this well is protected from infection.

Water in the future

As the people of the world continue to demand more water and climate change affects the distribution of water, the struggle to provide a sustainable supply of water will continue. With the technological developments of the last few decades, and increasing awareness of the solutions, it can be done. The UN still aims to halve the number of people who do not have access to clean, safe water by 2015. In the years following 2015, perhaps we will manage a fairer distribution of clean water around the world, and secure the supply for an equitable, safe future.

PERSPECTIVE

Water for all

'The potential exists to provide an adequate and sustainable supply of quality water for all, today and in the future. But there is no room for complacency. It is our common responsibility to take the challenge of today's global water crisis and address it in all of its aspects and dimensions.'

Jacques Diouf, Director-General, UN Food and Agriculture Organization

aquifer A natural underground water store in the form of rock, sand or clay which is soaked with water.

atmosphere The layer of gases (air) around a planet.

biodiversity The range of different animals and plants living in an environment.

borehole A narrow hole drilled into the ground, often to find or extract water.

canal An artificially made channel for water, either for delivering water or for transporting goods and people.

climate change Long-term changes in temperature and weather patterns.

cloud seeding Forcing rain to fall by making the droplets in a cloud fuse together until they are heavy enough to fall.

dam A barrier built across a river to block it and slow or stop the flow of water.

delta A triangular area of wetland, channels and small rivers formed where a river meets the sea and fans outs.

desertification The process of land changing into desert through drying out, heating up and losing its topsoil and plant cover.

drip irrigation A method of watering crops that uses a small amount of water, slowly delivered directly to the plants' roots.

drought A long period with little rain.

dry ice Carbon dioxide cooled to such a low temperature it has frozen solid.

estuary The place where a river meets the sea.

evaporate To turn from a liquid to a vapour.

famine An extreme shortage of food that leads to people starving.

fertilizer Substance used to improve the soil and promote plant growth.

fog harvesting Collecting water by condensing it from fog in the air.

fossil water Water which has been stored in closed underground aquifers for a very long time.

glacier A frozen river of ice.

global warming The increasing temperature of the air, sea and land caused by the build-up of greenhouse gases in the atmosphere.

greenhouse gases Gases which contribute to global warming by reflecting heat back to earth.

groundwater Water that is present under the ground, in soil and rock.

hydraulic engineering The branch of engineering that works with the flow and movement of liquids, especially water.

impermeable Not able to be penetrated by water.

International Monetary Fund A fund that lends money to countries on a short-term basis when they owe money to other countries.

irrigate To water crops.

meteoric water Water stored in underground aquifers that is part of the water cycle and renews itself relatively quickly.

organic pollutant Man-made organic compounds, usually made from carbon, which can pollute water.

polar ice sheet A large expanse of permanent ice at the North or South pole.

porous Allowing water to seep through.

privatization Transferring publicly owned resources from the government to private businesses.

reservoir A large body of water stored for people to use, generally in the form of a lake, pool or vast tank.

respiration The process of a plant or animal taking in oxygen from the air for use or growth, and expelling waste gases.

run-off Water which runs over the land rather than soaking in.

sluice A water channel controlled at its head by a gate.

sluice gate A gate used to control the water level in rivers or canals.

terraced field A field that allows people to grow crops on a hill. There is a series of flat platforms of soil on the side of the hill, which rise one above the other.

topsoil The layer of fertile soil rich in decayed animal and vegetable material which lies on top of rock, clay or sand and is needed for plants to grow.

water cycle The route water takes to be repeatedly recycled through clouds, rainwater, groundwater, rivers and the sea.

water footprint A measurement of water use. For example, a country's water footprint is the amount of fresh water used to produce the goods and services that it consumes. Poor countries can have a high water footprint because of water evaporation and a lack of water-saving measures.

water mining Drawing water from deep underground.

water table The level at which water is found underground (the top of the ground water layer).

water vapour Water existing in the air as a gas.

Website disclaimer
Note to parents and teachers: Every effort has been made by the publishers to ensure that these websites are suitable for children, that they are of the highest educational value, and that they contain no inappropriate or offensive material. However, because of the nature of the Internet, it is impossible to guarantee that the contents of these sites will not be altered. We strongly advise that Internet access is supervised by a responsible adult.

BOOKS

Earth Strikes Back: Water, Pamela Grant and Arthur Haswell, Chrysalis Children's Books, 2004

Environmental Issues: Water Pollution, Yael Calhoun, Chelsea House Publishers, 2005

Nature on the Rampage: Droughts, Duncan Scheff, Raintree, 2003

Nature's Changes: The Water Cycle, Bobbie Kalman and Rebecca Sjonger, Crabtree Publishing, 2006

Nature's Patterns: Water Cycle, Monica Hughes, Heinemann, 2005

Not a Drop to Drink: Water for a Thirsty World, Michael Burgin, National Geographic Society, 2008

Oceans and Rivers in Danger, Angela Royston, Heinemann, 2008

Our Earth: Saving Water, Peggy Hock, Children's Press, 2008

The Water Crisis, Craig Donnellan, Independence Educational Publishers, 2004

What If We Do Nothing: Water Supply, Rob Bowden, Franklin Watts, 2006

A Young People's Introduction: Sustainable Human Development, Peace Child International, Evans, 2003

WEBSITES

http://news.bbc.co.uk/1/hi/in_depth/world/2003/world_forum/water/default.stm
An in-depth look at many aspects of the water crisis.

http://vodpod.com/watch/259858-a-world-without-water-channel-4
A Channel 4 documentary about the water crisis.

www.un.org/waterforlifedecade/reference.html
Information about the United Nations 'Water for Life' programme.

www.waterfootprint.org/?page=files/home
Water footprints of nations and goods.

Page numbers in **BOLD** refer to illustrations and charts.